AUG. 11, 2005

2x 3/06

Black Bears

ABDO
Publishing Company

A Buddy Book
by
Julie Murray

VISIT US AT
www.abdopub.com

Published by Buddy Books, an imprint of ABDO Publishing Company, 4940 Viking Drive, Suite 622, Edina, Minnesota 55435. Copyright © 2005 by Abdo Consulting Group, Inc. International copyrights reserved in all countries. No part of this book may be reproduced in any form without written permission from the publisher.

Printed in the United States.

Edited by: Christy DeVillier
Contributing Editors: Matt Ray, Michael P. Goecke
Graphic Design: Maria Hosley
Image Research: Deborah Coldiron
Photographs: Corel, Mark Kostich, Minden Pictures

Library of Congress Cataloging-in-Publication Data

Murray, Julie, 1969-
  Black bears/Julie Murray.
    p. cm.—(Animal kingdom. Set II)
  Includes bibliographical references (p.).
  Contents: Bears—Black bears—Size and color—Where they live—Asiatic black bears —Hibernation—Food—Cubs—Black bear or brown bear?
  ISBN 1-59197-302-3
    1. Black bear—Juvenile literature. [1. Black bear. 2. Bears.] I. Title.

QL737.C27M8898 2003
599.78'5—dc21

2003040336

Contents

Bears 4

Black Bears 6

What They Look Like 8

Where They Live 11

Eating 14

Hibernation..16

Bear Cubs 18

Important Words 23

Web Sites 23

Index 24

Bears

Bears are the largest meat-eating, land animals around today. These strong animals can climb trees and run fast. Some bears can run as fast as 30 miles (48 km) per hour. Bears have a good sense of smell, too.

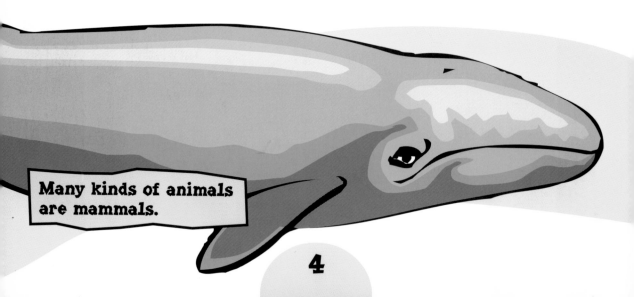

Many kinds of animals are mammals.

Bears are mammals. Mammals are born live instead of hatching from eggs. They use lungs to breathe air. Female mammals make milk in their bodies to feed their young. Most mammals have hair or fur instead of scales or feathers. Dogs, cats, apes, mice, whales, and people are mammals, too.

Black Bears

There are two kinds of black bears.
One kind is the American black bear.
It is the most common bear in
North America.

An American black bear

The second kind is the Asiatic black bear. Some people call it the moon bear. These bears have larger ears than the American black bear. The Asiatic bear also has a special mark on its chest. This mark looks like the letter *V*.

An Asiatic black bear baby

What They Look Like

Black bears walk on four legs. Sometimes, they stand up on their back feet. Each of their feet has five toes. Black bears have claws, too.

Black bears walk around on four legs.

Black bears grow to become as long as six feet (two m). American black bear adults weigh between 200 and 600 pounds (91 and 272 kg). They can grow heavier than Asiatic black bears. Some adult Asiatic black bears weigh less than 300 pounds (136 kg). Female black bears are smaller than males.

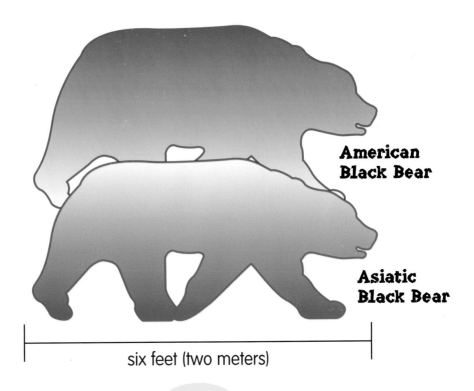

American Black Bear

Asiatic Black Bear

six feet (two meters)

Most black bears have a black coat with a brown muzzle. But not all black bears are black. Some have tan, reddish brown, gray, or white fur.

Some black bears are not black.

Where They Live

Black bears mostly stay in forests and wooded areas. Many live near mountains.

American black bears live in North America. They live in Canada, the United States, and northern Mexico. Many American black bears live in the Appalachian Mountains, the Rocky Mountains, and the Ozark Mountains.

The Asiatic black bear lives in many parts of Asia. They live in Pakistan, India, China, Vietnam, and many other countries.

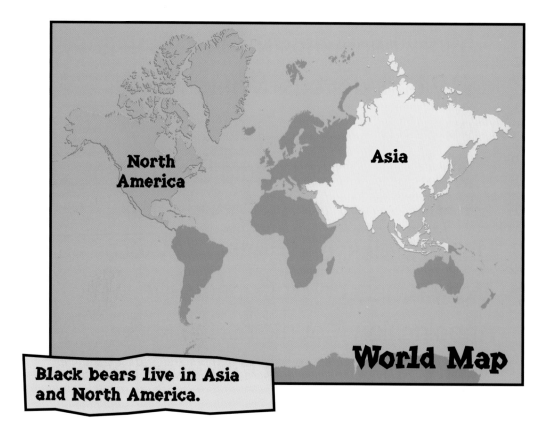

North America

Asia

World Map

Black bears live in Asia and North America.

Respect The Bears

Some black bears live near places where people camp. They have learned to look for food at campsites. Campers must store their food in a special way to keep bears away. Feeding bears is very dangerous. It is best to leave bears and other wild animals alone.

Some black bears look for food in trash.

Eating

Black bears eat both plants and animals. They eat berries, nuts, grass, roots, tree sap, and honey. A black bear will climb a tree to eat honey from a beehive. They may eat the whole beehive and the bees inside it, too.

This black bear has caught a fish.

Black bears eat small animals, such as mice. They catch and eat fish, too. Black bears also eat bigger animals, such as young moose and elk.

Hibernation

In the summer and fall, black bears eat a lot. All this food helps them build a lot of fat. Black bears live off this fat during the winter as they hibernate.

A hibernating bear does not eat. It spends three to seven months sleeping in its den. A bear's den can be a cave or a hollow log.

Mother bears hibernate with their cubs.

A black bear stops hibernating in the spring. It will wake up and leave its den. The hungry bear will begin looking for food.

Bear Cubs

Baby bears are called cubs. Female black bears commonly have two cubs at a time. Cubs are born in the mother's den when she is hibernating. This commonly happens in January or February.

A black bear cub

Newborn cubs are small and helpless. They drink their mother's milk for many months.

This black bear cub
is looking for food.

Cubs leave their dens in the spring. Mother black bears teach their cubs how to find food. After about 18 months, young black bears are ready to live on their own. They may live as long as 25 years.

By the age of 18 months, many black bears are on their own.

Important Words

den a special, hidden place for bears to hibernate.

hibernate to spend the winter sleeping.

mammal most living things that belong to this special group have hair, give birth to live babies, and make milk to feed their babies.

muzzle the nose and mouth area.

Web Sites

To learn more about black bears, visit ABDO Publishing Company on the World Wide Web. Web sites about black bears are featured on our Book Links page. These links are routinely monitored and updated to provide the most current information available.

www.abdopub.com

Index

American black bears **6, 7, 9, 11**

apes **5**

Appalachian Mountains **11**

Asia **12**

Asiatic black bears **7, 9, 12**

beehive **14**

berries **14**

Canada **11**

cats **5**

China **12**

claws **8**

coat **10**

cubs **17, 18, 19, 20, 21**

den **16, 17, 18, 21**

dogs **5**

elk **15**

fat **16**

fish **15**

fur **10**

grass **14**

hibernate **16, 17**

honey **14**

India **12**

legs **8**

mammals **4, 5**

Mexico **11**

mice **5, 15**

moon bear **7**

moose **15**

muzzle **10**

North America **6, 11, 12**

nuts **14**

Ozark Mountains **11**

Pakistan **12**

Rocky Mountains **11**

roots **14**

toes **8**

tree sap **14**

United States **11**

Vietnam **12**

whales **5**